Join the conversation on Twitter using #CSuite and share your own business insider tips with us @CSNAdvisors or @CSuiteNetwork.

C-Suite Executives' Guide to Success

Powerful Tips from C-Suite Network Advisors to Become a More Effective C-Suite Executive

Lindsey Hayzlett
and Mitchell Levy

Foreword by
Jeffrey Hayzlett

THiNKaha®

An Actionable Business Journal

E-mail: info@thinkaha.com
20660 Stevens Creek Blvd., Suite 210
Cupertino, CA 95014

⇨ Please go to **http://aha.pub/CSuiteExecutivesGuide** to read this AHAbook and to share the individual AHAmessages that resonate with you.

Published by THiNKaha®
20660 Stevens Creek Blvd., Suite 210, Cupertino, CA 95014
http://thinkaha.com
E-mail: **info@thinkaha.com**

First Printing: November 2018
Hardcover ISBN: 978-1-61699-302-3 1-61699-302-2
Paperback ISBN: 978-1-61699-301-6 1-61699-301-4
eBook ISBN: 978-1-61699-300-9 1-61699-300-6
Place of Publication: Silicon Valley, California, USA
Paperback Library of Congress Number: 2018962421

Acknowledgement

BIG thanks to:

Co-author, Mitchell Levy, who took on the task of connecting with all of these great minds to provide a book that offered key takeaways and solutions to real business problems we go through every day.

Lindsey Hayzlett, the co-author of this book for her dedication to our C-Suite Network Advisors and working to create this opportunity to highlight them.

The C-Suite Network team members Ashley Knapp, McKenzie Holton, Cathi Jo McGee, and Keira Rodriguez, who have helped produce this book.

To all of the talented and brilliant contributors: our C-Suite Network Advisors, members, and executives. Without your knowledge and expertise, this book wouldn't be possible.

How to Read a THiNKaha® Book

A Note from the Publisher

The AHAthat/THiNKaha series is the CliffsNotes of the 21st century. These books are contextual in nature. Although the actual words won't change, their meaning will every time you read one as your context will change. Be ready, you will experience your own AHA moments as you read the AHA messages™ in this book. They are designed to be stand-alone actionable messages that will help you think about a project you're working on, an event, a sales deal, a personal issue, etc. differently. As you read this book, please think about the following:

1. It should only take 15–20 minutes to read this book the first time out. When you're reading, write in the underlined area one to three action items that resonate with you.
2. Mark your calendar to re-read this book again in 30 days.
3. Repeat step #1 and mark one to three more AHA messages that resonate. They will most likely be different than the first time. BTW: this is also a great time to reflect on the AHAmessages that resonated with you during your last reading.

After reading a THiNKaha book, marking your AHA messages, re-reading it, and marking more AHA messages, you'll begin to see how these books contextually apply to you. AHAthat/ THiNKaha books advocate for continuous, lifelong learning. They will help you transform your AHAs into actionable items with tangible results until you no longer have to say AHA to these moments—they'll become part of your daily practice as you continue to grow and learn.

Mitchell Levy, The AHA Guy at AHAthat
publisher@thinkaha.com

THiNKaha®

Contents

Foreword

How do you define success? What does success mean to you? The word itself means different things to different people. It's not about right or wrong, it's just different. For some, success is measured by money, titles, a corner office, a successful work-life integration, or even flexibility in work hours. Whatever your metric is, it's yours and yours alone. No one can take that away from you.

The 'c-suite' is also synonymous with corner offices, high salaries, big responsibilities, and the pressure to constantly perform, deliver big results, and withstand public scrutiny. The road to the c-suite isn't smooth, and it's not meant to be. However, that doesn't mean that you can't learn from someone else's tribulations on your way there.

This book is a compilation of tips and advice from some of the most trusted and wise minds in business today, which also include 'hero' leaders. Those who contributed to this book have faced a multitude of road bumps on their way to the top in their pursuit of excellence. Let their experience be your true north as they help you navigate the rough seas in route to your success.

The life of an entrepreneur can be a lonely and isolated one. The book serves as a reminder that we're not alone in this journey and that we have a team of people willing to guide and drive us through this road. As a community that prides itself in being a resource to others while providing value and community, I hope the advice you find here will encourage you to always strive for bigger and better things. After all, it takes guts to get the glory!

Jeffrey Hayzlett
Chairman & CEO, C-Suite Network

It's not who you are that's holding you back, it's who you think you're not. You have to believe in yourself and let your strong will to achieve success burn brightly.
#UnlockYourPotential #CSuite
@CSuiteNetwork @CSNAdvisors
http://aha.pub/MitchellLevy
http://aha.pub/CSuiteExecutivesGuide

Share the AHA messages from this book socially by going to http://aha.pub/CSuiteExecutivesGuide.

Section I

Unlocking Your Full Potential

Many people strive to unlock their full potential in order to achieve greater things in life. The key to unlocking your potential lies within you. You need to develop yourself as a person and grow stronger mentally and emotionally. Open your mind and heart to have more effective relationships with the people around you who can help achieve your goals.

As a C-Suite Executive, remember that success starts with you. How you think, how you feel, and how you act greatly determines you and your company's future.

1

In order to be successful,
you have to define what it means to you,
and you're the only one who can do that.
Define it, strive for it, live it.
—Jeffrey Hayzlett

______

______

______

2

It's not who you are that's holding you back,
it's who you think you're not. You have to
believe in yourself and let your strong will
to achieve success burn brightly.
—Mitchell Levy

3

Think bigger. Don't be constrained by where you are now or what's been done before. Set the groundwork for incredible success. Then get out of the way.
—Linda Popky

___

___

___

4

Do your own personal growth work; know your blindspots so others don't know more about you than you know about yourself. How much do you know yourself?

—Tina Greenbaum

5

Master your weaknesses
and turn them into your strengths.
—Michelle Nasser

6

Listen more, be open to new ideas that
aren't yours, and be a lifelong learner.
—Julie Ann Sullivan

7

In times of adversity, be strong enough to stand, smart enough to know when you need help, and brave enough to ask for it.

—Matt Sweetwood

8

Don't always go with your brain. Sometimes let your heart rule your decisions.
—Matt Sweetwood

9

You own your story.
Take control of your own narrative.
—Dr. Rachel MK Headley

10

The way you start your morning sets the tone of how you play out the rest of your day. Master your Morning!
—Dr. Karen Jacobson

11

Everyone struggles with imposter syndrome at some point. Forget "Fake it 'til you make it." No one wants to be a fake.
Instead, "Act it... and become it."
—Jess Todtfeld

12

Behave, think, and feel
(and insist that all others do too)
as if the desired future were already here.
—Blaine Bartlett

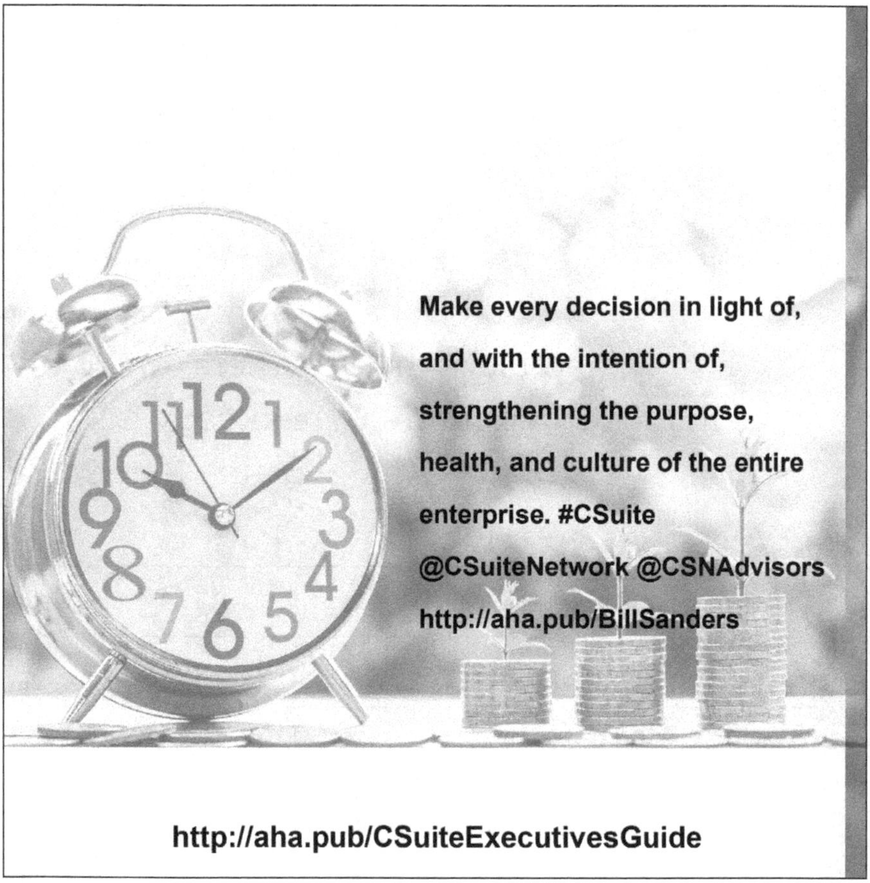
Make every decision in light of, and with the intention of, strengthening the purpose, health, and culture of the entire enterprise. #CSuite
@CSuiteNetwork @CSNAdvisors
http://aha.pub/BillSanders
http://aha.pub/CSuiteExecutivesGuide

Share the AHA messages from this book socially by going to http://aha.pub/CSuiteExecutivesGuide.

Section II

How to Be a More Effective C-Suite Executive

How effective you are at the things you do greatly determines the future of your business. With all the things that can deter you from being efficient and effective, it can be troublesome to always stay focused and make the best decisions possible.

In this section, you'll learn that even the smallest things you do each day can help you be at your absolute best.

13

Ask yourself one question every day:
"How badly do you want to succeed?"
—Matt Sweetwood

14

Bring your personal best each day,
realizing your personal best
may vary from day to day.
—Sheila A. Anderson

15

You cannot afford to not be at your best every day. Leadership self-care is the foundation for sustainable success and burnout prevention.
—Jeanette Bronee

16

Stay present.
Don't let your attention stray or drift.
Stay in the moment
and anchored within your body.
—Casey Carpenter

17

Spend time for personal development
and planning daily.
Don't get caught up in the tasks of the day.
—Mari Anne Vanella

18

Surround yourself with people who excel in areas you don't. If you're the smartest person in the room, you won't experience the same growth as you would surrounded by those who know more than you.

—Dr. Diane Hamilton

19

List 3 things you will achieve today, no matter what daily business or urgent fires that arise. Act on the phenomenal power that you have in order to do things that can lead to your greatness each day.
—Tricia Benn

20

Procrastination will destroy your dreams.
Don't do it.
—Chris Rabalais

21

Stay focused on your 3–4 critical goals, and don't get caught up in the surrounding noise. What are your critical goals?
—Daniel Elliott

22

To be more effective at what you do,
have someone tell you the truth
about your performance and
give you honest feedback.
—Marty Wolff

23

Be as clear as possible in all your written
and verbal communications.
Are you communicating clearly?
—Patricia Iyer

24

Market with your mouth.
Speaking is your #1 tool to expand
your influence, increase sales,
and strengthen your culture.
—David Newman

25

Einstein said that if he only had 1 hour to solve a problem, he would spend 55 minutes defining the problem and 5 minutes solving it. Thoughtful inquiry enables you to determine the next best step to make.
—Lisa Nirell

26

Improvise! The most successful executives are willing to adapt, be flexible, and change the rules in the face of disruption.
Be willing to play and think upside down when the strategic plan won't work.
—Karen Hough

27

Don't let your business compromise your health, or your health might end up compromising your business.
—Jeanette Bronee

28

Make every decision in light of, and with the intention of, strengthening the purpose, health, and culture of the entire enterprise.
—Bill Sanders

Show up strong. Be yourself and practice! The reason executives lack presence is because they forget to practice impact in small and large interactions, and forget to be intentional about the impression they leave. #CSuite @CSuiteNetwork @CSNAdvisors http://aha.pub/KarenHough
http://aha.pub/CSuiteExecutivesGuide

Share the AHA messages from this book socially by going to http://aha.pub/CSuiteExecutivesGuide.

Section III

Leading Your Company to Success

C-Suite Executives often have a lot on their plate—from being the rainmaker of their business to effectively leading the people in their company. How can you lead your company to your desired goal?

First, you need to be conscious of the way you talk and act. You need to demonstrate executive presence to command respect and inspire others. When you lead your team members instead of just managing them, you'll be able to impart your passion and vision, making them even more motivated to help bring your company to success.

29

Show up strong. Be yourself and practice!
The reason executives lack presence is
because they forget to practice impact in
small and large interactions,
and forget to be intentional about
the impression they leave.
—Karen Hough

30

Be able to command respect and inspire trust to enroll others in your vision.
—Diane DiResta

31

Think about the way you think. If you possess too much rigidity in your thought process, you'll miss opportunities that might flow from unsuspecting sources.
—Greg Williams

32

To be the best place to buy from,
you need to be the best place to work at.
Take care of your employees,
and they will take care of your customers.
—Shep Hyken

33

Only in community do we have the
resources to help everyone succeed.
How are you creating your community?
—Julie Ann Sullivan

34

Be a great listener,
be open to new ideas, and give your
workforce the tools to succeed.
—Julie Ann Sullivan

35

Keep an open mind when it comes to innovative ideas. Too many people are afraid to pose suggestions or ask questions for fear of looking like they don't know as much as they should.
—Dr. Diane Hamilton

36

It's human nature to want to be heard. Make sure you have a system in place that allows for your employees to have a voice.
—Tina Greenbaum

37

Listen for why someone might be right, not wrong. Which are you listening to?
—Evan Hackel

38

Executives are always negotiating. Thus, the casual dismissal of a question/suggestion or the embrace of it can alter the direction of the organization. How do you handle questions/suggestions?
—Greg Williams

39

If you want to see accountability,
demonstrate it first. Develop your ability
to keep your agreements
if you expect your team to keep theirs.
—Wally Hauck

40

Customer service is not a department—
it's a philosophy to be embraced
by every employee, from the CEO
to the most recently hired employee.
—Shep Hyken

41

Everyone is measured and accountable to the customer. Create divisional or segmented customer value councils, and drive innovation faster.
—Edward Golod

42

Make your processes simple and practical
as much as possible—
easy to understand and use.
—Tony Alessandra

43

Learn who your high-value customers are, where to find them, and how to keep them in order to help you successfully guide your customer service teams and clarify which product features should be built first.
—Allison Hartsoe

44

Technology is a tool to drive value creation and business growth. Remember that equal attention to "people" and "processes" are important in order to maximize enterprise value and business growth.

—Todd Williams

45

In less than 5 years, EVERY business should be a technology-led business. What is your digital strategy and execution plan to create enterprise value, accelerate growth, and remain relevant?
—Todd Williams

46

Transform your sales and marketing teams and the company on customer value delivery to gain your key competitive advantage.

—Edward Golod

47

Create a data-driven culture that uses analytics and technology to make the right marketing decisions quickly.
—Mike Moran

48

Invest your clients through story, to care about your data!
—Mikki Williams

49

What if your company was not just data-driven but also customer-driven? Delighting high-value customers not only creates a 10x return on investment but also ignites a virtuous cycle of recurring value and focus.

—Allison Hartsoe

50

Recognize and appreciate how your org is a social system. The parts of your org are interdependent and influence each other to be either engaged or indifferent.
—Wally Hauck

51

We naively assume any group can automatically be a team. But actually, one of the biggest single reasons that teams misfire and miscommunicate is that personality differences are ignored.
—Tony Alessandra

52

Culture trumps all!
The culture of your company will be defined by the worst possible behavior that you, the CEO, tolerate from any one employee.
—Bill Wallace

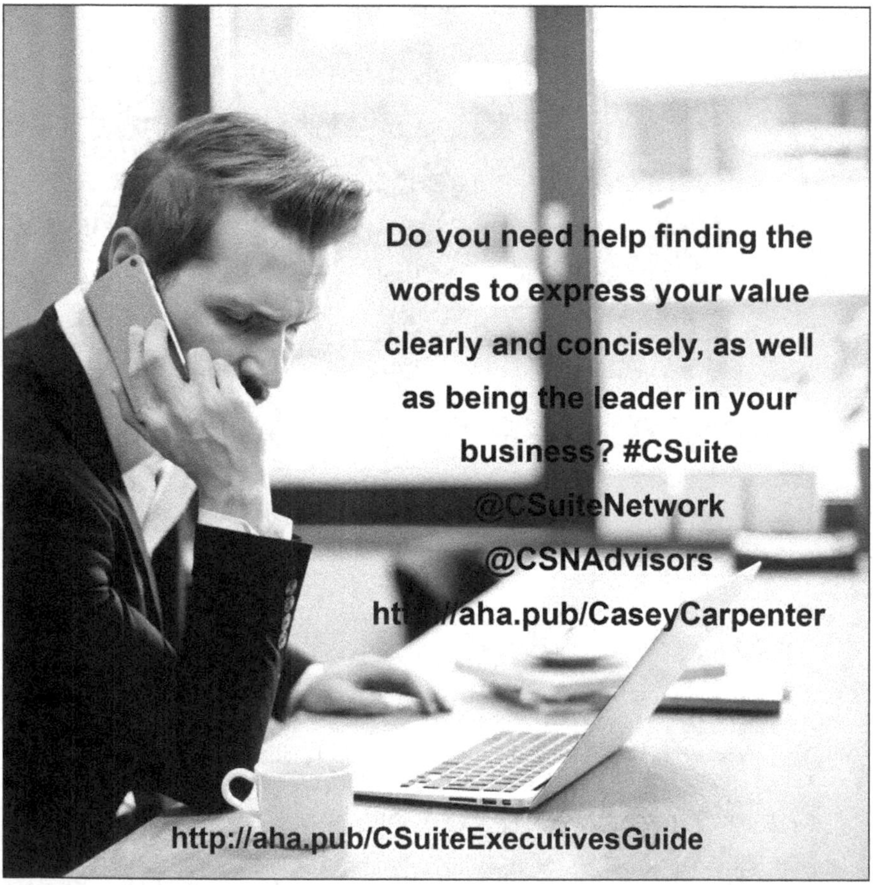
Do you need help finding the words to express your value clearly and concisely, as well as being the leader in your business? #CSuite
@CSuiteNetwork
@CSNAdvisors
http://aha.pub/CaseyCarpenter
http://aha.pub/CSuiteExecutivesGuide

Share the AHA messages from this book socially by going to
http://aha.pub/CSuiteExecutivesGuide.

Section IV

When to Seek Help from C-Suite Network Advisors

Managing a business is never easy; there are many problems that can come up at any given time, which can cause you to feel stuck. Are you unable to get your team aligned with your vision? Do you feel like you're not doing enough to help your company succeed? These are just a few of the problems you'll encounter as a C-Suite Executive.

When you feel like you're stuck, you need to have the right people around who can help you get "unstuck." Always remember that you are not alone; there are always people who can help you. Be brave enough to admit that you need help and have the courage to ask for it.

53

Do you need help finding the words to express your value clearly and concisely, as well as being the leader in your business?
—Casey Carpenter

54

Do you want to be effective in managing
a large scope of relationships
that you don't see in person?
Do you want to feel comfortable starting
and managing long-term relationships
that turn into revenue remotely?
—Mari Anne Vanella

55

Is your business thriving
but your personal life is suffering?
—Tina Greenbaum

56

Are your top line goals not being met, and you don't have the luxury of time to figure this out?
—Edward Golod

57

Do you need help identifying and evaluating the best options for you to make the greatest impact on your organization?
—Michelle Nasser

58

Are you clear on your strategy but still haven't bridged the execution gap between it and the results you anticipated?
—Bill Sanders

59

Is your business data-rich but information-poor? Do you want to know how to extract value from your data and transform/grow your business concurrent with remaining competitive in the market?
—Todd Williams

60

Do you want to know the value of having a great negotiator on your team?
—Greg Williams

61

Why wait for the pain? Dig your well before you're thirsty. Who in advance do you want to assemble as your advisory team to meet, advise, and coach to their expertise?

—Shep Hyken

62

Do you need to strengthen the core leaders in your organization to be better able to influence your teams, execute your mission, and develop your people?
—Ed Brzychcy

63

Do you feel like you make most decisions alone? Is there no one you could trust to make the best decisions?

—Matt Sweetwood

64

Do you have a problem in your team getting things done but can't put your finger on how to fix it?
—Dr. Rachel MK Headley

65

Is your company losing productivity and profit due to employee eldercare challenges?
—Derrick McDaniel

66

Wouldn't it be great if you could find someone to coach the people you can't seem to reach?

—Daniel Elliott

67

Do you have someone who'll work with leaders on adapting their communication style so they can more easily connect with all their direct reports?
—Tony Alessandra

68

Would you like to know how to get your team to bring it all together to become more productive?
—Dr. Diane Hamilton

69

Are you often baffled and frustrated about your team not performing and exerting as much effort as you are?
—Wally Hauck

70

Do you want someone to train your staff how to settle negotiation strategies and tactics that work at the negotiation table?
—Greg Williams

71

Do you find yourself taking too long to make a decision?
—Marty Wolff

72

Are you too busy putting out fires and not moving forward? Do you feel like you've been steady but are not growing?
—Dr. Karen Jacobson

73

Is your company about to grow exponentially and you're afraid that you have no idea how to manage the growth?
—Frumi Rachel Barr

74

Are you looking to level up your business? Are you doing well but want to go to the next level?
—Evan Hackel

75

Do you want to increase your visibility and influence by establishing yourself as a thought leader in your industry?
—Sheila A. Anderson

Feeling stuck? Have someone work with you to help get you to see past yourself. #CSuite
@CSuiteNetwork
@CSNAdvisors
http://aha.pub/JessTodtfeld
http://aha.pub/CSuiteExecutivesGuide

Share the AHA messages from this book socially by going to http://aha.pub/CSuiteExecutivesGuide.

Section V

How C-Suite Network Advisors Can Help You

C-Suite Network Advisors are people you can turn to for help when you have problems in your business. Their job is to help C-Suite Executives like yourself succeed in what you do, as well as help you grow your company.

In this section, you'll learn about common problems that many C-Suite Executives face today and how C-Suite Network Advisors can help.

76

Feeling stuck? Have someone work with you to help get you to see past yourself.
—Jess Todtfeld

77

Are you struggling to stay on top of your busy schedule and losing your edge? Pause for lunch for 30 minutes every day to have more energy, better focus, and increase your productivity.
—Jeanette Bronee

78

Always feeling overwhelmed? Have someone help you track your hours each week to discover if you're making the best use of your time.

—Lisa Nirell

79

Do you need a major change but are not sure if you can pull it off? Have someone analyze your skills from an external perspective to determine if you can or can't make the changes you need to do.

—Dr. Rachel MK Headley

80

Having trouble getting your key messages across to bring in more business? Have someone help and coach you on how to refine your communication skills.
—Diane DiResta

81

Are your clients leaving you due to lack of diversity? Have someone create an inclusive approach to your everyday communication and operational actions to improve your retention rate.

—Karen Hough

82

Are you speaking and presenting a lot but not getting as much attention as you expected? Have someone help you build a communication strategy and create a clear, specific call-to-action.

—David Newman

83

Are your investments failing to deliver targeted new account wins? Have someone help you deploy a business outcome sales and marketing strategy to increase your chances of closing more deals.
—Edward Golod

84

Don't know whether you should continue to invest in a particular market or just cut your losses? Have someone help you evaluate the market and guide you on where you should focus and where you should cut back.

—Linda Popky

85

Still not ready to make a big investment? Have someone convince you by showing you several small investments that will provide immediate impact.
—Mike Moran

86

Do you need to have a crucial conversation with an executive who's not getting the message of what was expected? Have someone help push you to talk to the executive NOW rather than later.

—Daniel Elliott

87

Do you generate massive amounts of data from multiple sources but don't have any productization strategy in place? Have someone help you prioritize the data and create a strategy around it to generate more revenue.
—Todd Williams

88

Looking for additional ways to expand the reach of your company brand? Have someone help you focus on building your personal brand and tie it back to the brand, since you are the face of your company.

—Sheila A. Anderson

89

Planning on creating an ideal team environment? Have someone start planning around the team you have today to set realistic plans in motion.
—Mari Anne Vanella

90

Want to increase the effectivity and efficiency of your team? Have someone shift your mindset from management to leadership in order to empower your company to play to their strengths.

—Dr. Karen Jacobson

91

Are your employees' productivity decreasing due to eldercare issues? Have someone help you understand why it's happening and teach you how to recognize and support distressed employees.
—Derrick McDaniel

92

Are you struggling with customer retention? Have someone help your employees recognize the role they play in taking care of the customers.
—Shep Hyken

93

Fixated on just a single solution to address a challenge? Have someone help you alter your paradigm to see more possible options.
—Greg Williams

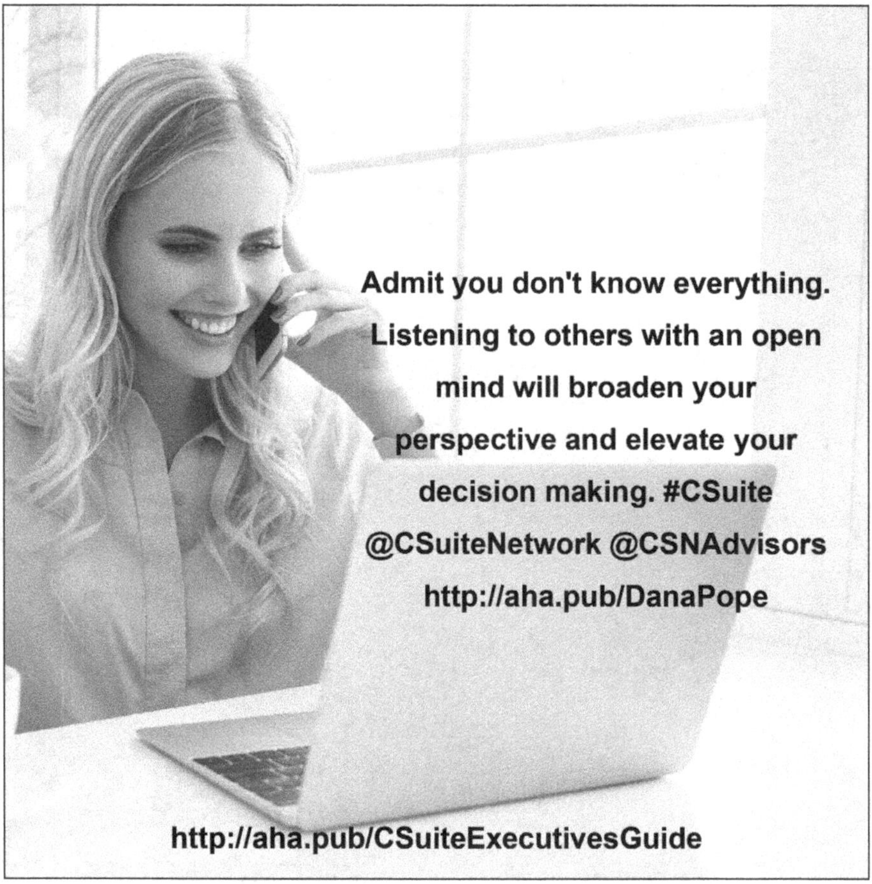
Admit you don't know everything.
Listening to others with an open mind will broaden your perspective and elevate your decision making. #CSuite @CSuiteNetwork @CSNAdvisors http://aha.pub/DanaPope
http://aha.pub/CSuiteExecutivesGuide

Share the AHA messages from this book socially by going to http://aha.pub/CSuiteExecutivesGuide.

Section VI

Actionable Pieces of Advice That Can Change Your Day

Your effectiveness and efficiency depend on what you do each day. If you start the day in a bad mood, your performance as a leader can be affected, and it can also affect the performance of your team. On the other hand, if you start your day in a good mood, you're sure to be more effective and efficient at work.

Here are actionable pieces of advice given by C-Suite Network Advisors that can help you master your day to make sure you're at your very best.

94

Always start your day with a smile. When you smile, not only do you put yourself in a good mood, but so will other people you interact with. When there's positivity, everyone becomes more productive and efficient.
—Mitchell Levy

95

Ground energy with a short meditation that will help with focus and being present.

—Diane DiResta

96

Skip the coffee and drink more water. How many glasses of water do you drink every day?
—Jeanette Bronee

97

Create healthy routines around your diet, exercise, sleep, spiritual practice, and relationships. Be prudent with your use of digital devices. The rest will fall into place.
—Lisa Nirell

98

Move through your day with conviction, compassion, and consistency.
—Daniel Elliott

99

You might fool other people but don't fool yourself! Be who you really are.
—Frumi Rachel Barr

100

Have a plan for the day! Don't rely on routine. What's your plan today?
—Mari Anne Vanella

101

Know the one thing you have to accomplish today, and make sure you have time available in your schedule to complete it.
—Bill Sanders

102

Write three priorities to accomplish for the day first thing in the morning or the night before, and then do those things first. That's the key to feeling the day was a productive one.
—Frumi Rachel Barr

103

The purpose of goals is to grow. Be sure the goals you're setting are uncomfortable and can stretch you and your organization into areas not yet experienced or explored.

—Blaine Bartlett

104

Eat the frog.
Do the things you hate the most first.
—Chris Rabalais

105

When you're feeling stuck, don't stay there—take action or get support or both!
—Kelli Richards

106

Take the time to proofread anything you write, and have another person proof it as well. Mistakes can have long-lasting consequences.

—Patricia Iyer

107

Before sending an email, stop, breathe, and ponder if there is a way to cut down the words to improve clarity. Don't write emails when angry. Proofread, then send.

—Patricia Iyer

108

Video, video, video! You're the best possible messenger of your company's message, so get on camera NOW.
—David Newman

109

Do not start your presentations with "good morning, thanks for inviting me," etc. Start with a story, a quote, a statistic, a name, a date, or a place.

—Mikki Williams

110

Focus on areas that have been overlooked. Everything counts when you want to drive sales from digital marketing, not just the sexy parts that everyone is talking about.
—Mike Moran

111

Succeed fast: Run fast, take a breath, and iterate. Competitors spur us on and challenge us to reach further; time is the real enemy.
—Tricia Benn

112

Execution makes the difference between market leaders and laggards, but it requires coordinated focus. What are the 3 or 4 metrics that, if achieved, would create undeniable success?
—Allison Hartsoe

113

Celebrate small victories. We work so hard to achieve goals. When we achieve them, we often don't stop and recognize the moment. It's like a race without a finish line.

—Jess Todtfeld

114

You represent your brand. Make sure your actions and decisions are congruent with the brand and culture you want to build.

—Linda Popky

115

Be visible and authentic in your interactions with your employees. Are you visible and authentic?
—Tina Greenbaum

116

Be authentic. That means to speak
authentically, lead authentically,
and sell authentically.
—Casey Carpenter

117

Express sincere appreciation to everyone with whom you interact. Do it for an hour, then a day, then a week, then always.
—Wally Hauck

118

Practice acknowledgment, and constantly look for ways to acknowledge people.

—Evan Hackel

119

Be curious: Ask everyone you meet today a question about something they do, to find out more about them and their projects.
—Dr. Diane Hamilton

120

Listen more than you talk today. Use open-ended questions to elicit information, and rather than responding or judging, think about it for 24 hours first.
—Karen Hough

121

Listen from a place of curiosity, not judgment; that's when great ideas are brought to life.

—Evan Hackel

122

Admit you don't know everything. Listening to others with an open mind will broaden your perspective and elevate your decision making.

—Dana Pope

123

Recognize that every interaction you make is an opportunity to learn something new.

—Michelle Nasser

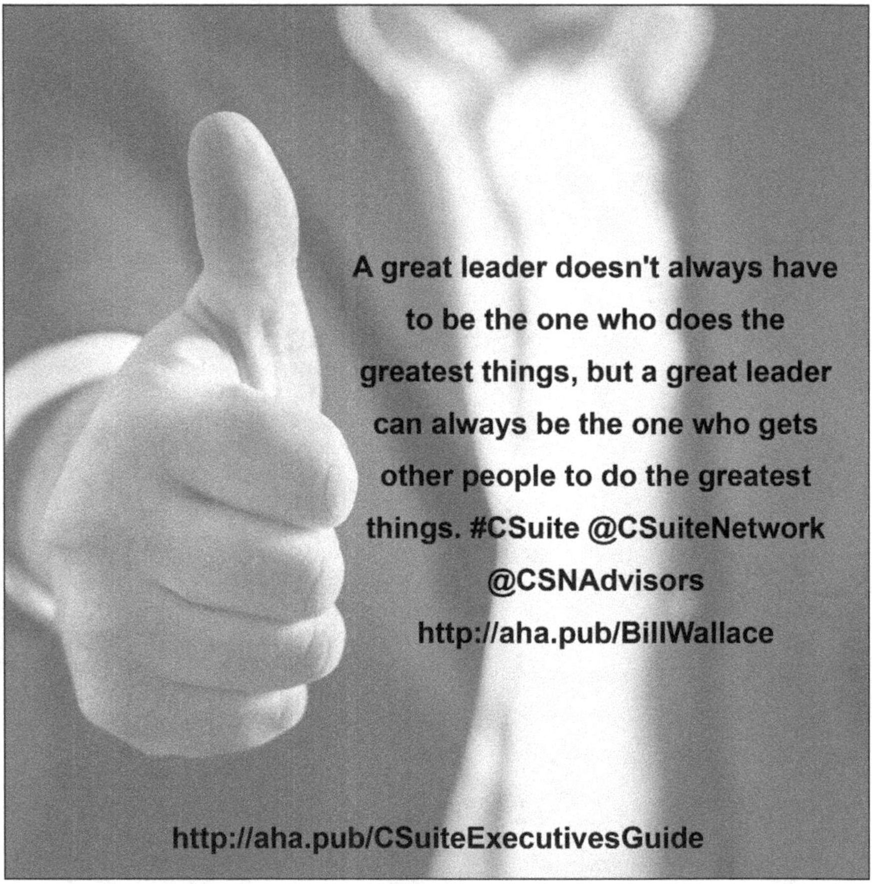
A great leader doesn't always have to be the one who does the greatest things, but a great leader can always be the one who gets other people to do the greatest things. #CSuite @CSuiteNetwork @CSNAdvisors http://aha.pub/BillWallace
http://aha.pub/CSuiteExecutivesGuide

Share the AHA messages from this book socially by going to http://aha.pub/CSuiteExecutivesGuide.

Section VII

Conclusion

Being an effective C-Suite Executive can be extremely difficult; you always need to be at your best. However, we are only human and we're prone to get stuck at times, and that's okay. Always remember that even leaders need help sometimes.

Learn to embrace your flaws—don't run away from them. Look at everything in life as an opportunity to learn and grow. Success starts with you, and how you look at all the good and not-so-good things in your business can greatly determine the success of your company.

124

Success means different things for different people. Whatever your definition is, it's yours and yours alone. No one can tell you it's wrong. What's your definition of success?
—Jeffrey Hayzlett

125

Success can be defined by your conditions
of satisfaction. Mine are: to make money,
learn something new,
and have fun in the process.
What are your conditions of satisfaction?
—Jeffrey Hayzlett

126

Create the life you want to live,
then build your career around THAT.
—Lisa Nirell

127

Every so often during the day, ask yourself, "What am I doing and why am I doing it?"

—Chris Rabalais

128

Set goals that will stretch you to your current limit. Don't be afraid to take risks. Learn to recognize opportunities, and be brave enough to pursue them.

—Mitchell Levy

129

Embrace the 4 F's: flaws, feedback, failure, and fear. Turn these dreaded four into the fabulous four! Look at everything in life as an opportunity to learn and grow.
—Dr. Karen Jacobson

130

Don't be cowed by the experts. You don't have to be an expert in analytics or technology; find experts who speak to you in business terms. If they are confusing you, you have the wrong experts.

—Mike Moran

131

When you've created your company and have a vision for it, know how to get it there so no one could shake you from that objective. You can't please everyone, but then again, everyone is not your target customer.
—Dana Pope

132

In storytelling, relive, don't retell. You'll be able to communicate more effectively.
—Mikki Williams

133

Build trusted long-term relationships with your clients where you both look out for each other's well-being authentically and deliver value.
—Kelli Richards

134

Always be kind. Karma really does exist.
—Marty Wolff

135

Remember that the words "react"
and "create" have the same letters;
we get to choose whether we're a "reactor"
or a "creator" in life.
—Kelli Richards

136

Lead with purpose: Set the standard for your organization, drive the business's culture, and do not be afraid to get your hands dirty.
—Ed Brzychcy

137

Don't wish to have your name on
the office door or on an office building.
Wish for your name to be on the hearts of
your family, friends, team,
business partners, and customers.
—Marty Wolff.

138

Be memorable. Too many businesses and
people are forgettable. Stand out!
—Jess Todtfeld

139

Develop the mindset that "It" has already happened, we just haven't arrived yet!
—Blaine Bartlett

140

A great leader doesn't always have to be the one who does the greatest things, but a great leader can always be the one who gets other people to do the greatest things.

—Bill Wallace

Appendix

Contributors

Name of Contributor	Title	AHA #
Allison Hartsoe https://www.linkedin.com/in/allisonhartsoe	CEO of Ambition Data LLC	43, 49, 112
Bill Sanders https://www.linkedin.com/in/thebillsanders/	Principal & Managing Director of Roebling Strauss Inc.	28, 58, 101
Bill Wallace https://www.linkedin.com/in/billwallace1	Founder of Success North Dallas	52, 140
Blaine Bartlett https://www.linkedin.com/in/blainebartlett/	President & CEO of Avatar Resources	12, 103, 139
Casey Carpenter https://www.linkedin.com/in/caseycarpenter1/	CEO of The Sales Breakthrough	16, 53, 116
Chris Rabalais https://www.linkedin.com/in/chrisrabalais/	Co-Founder of AllSportsMarket	20, 104, 127
Daniel Elliott https://www.linkedin.com/in/rdanielelliott/	Managing Director of E3 Strategy Development LLC	21, 66, 86, 98
Dana Pope https://www.linkedin.com/in/popedana/	Owner of Dana Lynn Pope LLC	122, 131
David Newman https://www.linkedin.com/in/davidjnewman/	Founder of Do It! Marketing	24, 82, 108
Derrick McDaniel https://www.linkedin.com/in/mreldercare101/	CEO of Mr. Eldercare 101 Enterprises Inc.	65, 91
Diane DiResta https://www.linkedin.com/in/dianediresta/	Founder of DiResta Communications, Inc.	30, 80, 95
Dr. Diane Hamilton https://www.linkedin.com/in/drdianehamilton/	Founder at Tonerra - Business Behavioral Expert	18, 35, 68, 119
Ed Brzychcy https://www.linkedin.com/in/ebrzychcy/	Founder at Blue Cord Management LLC	62, 136
Edward Golod https://www.linkedin.com/in/edwardgolod/	CEO & Founder of Revenue Accelerators	41, 46, 56, 83
Evan Hackel https://www.linkedin.com/in/evanhackel/	CEO of Ingage Consulting and Tortal Training	37, 74, 118, 121
Frumi Rachel Barr https://www.linkedin.com/in/frumirachelbarr/	Chief Inspiration Officer at Scollar Inc.	73, 99, 102
Greg Williams https://www.linkedin.com/in/themasternegotiator/	The Master Negotiator & Body Language Expert	31, 38, 60, 70, 93
Jeanette Bronée https://www.linkedin.com/in/jeanettebronee/	CEO, Founder, and Performance Strategist	15, 27, 77, 96
Jeffrey Hayzlett https://www.linkedin.com/in/hayzlett/	Chairman & CEO, C-Suite Network	1, 124, 125
Jess Todtfeld, CSP https://www.linkedin.com/in/Todtfeld/	President of Results First Training/Success in Media	11, 76, 113, 138
Julie Ann Sullivan https://www.linkedin.com/in/julieannsullivan/	Business Culture Expert	6, 33, 34
Karen Hough https://www.linkedin.com/in/karenhoughimprov	Founder and CEO of ImprovEdge	26, 29, 81, 120

Dr. Karen Jacobson https://www.linkedin.com/in/drkarenjacobson/	High-Performance Strategist	10, 72, 90, 129
Kelli Richards https://www.linkedin.com/in/kellirichards/	CEO & President of the All Access Group LLC	105, 133, 135
Linda Popky https://www.linkedin.com/in/lindapopky/	President of Leverage2Market Associates	3, 84, 114
Lisa Nirell https://www.linkedin.com/in/energizegrowth/	Chief Energy Officer of Energize Growth LLC.	25, 78, 97, 126
Mari Anne Vanella https://www.linkedin.com/in/vanellagroup/	CEO of The Vanella Group Inc.	17, 54, 89, 100
Marty Wolff https://www.linkedin.com/in/martywolffceo/	CEO of Marty Wolff Business Solutions	22, 71, 134, 137
Matt Sweetwood https://www.linkedin.com/in/msweetwood/	The CEO Coach	7, 8, 13, 63
Michelle Nasser https://www.linkedin.com/in/michellenasser-04043/?originalSubdomain=ca	President of Michelle Nasser Group Intl.	5, 57, 123
Mike Moran https://www.linkedin.com/in/mikemoran/	President of Mike Moran Group LLC	47, 85, 110, 130
Mikki Williams https://www.linkedin.com/in/mikkiwilliams/	Hall of Fame speaker, executive speech coach, Master Chair Vistage Worldwide	48, 109, 132
Mitchell Levy https://www.linkedin.com/in/mitchelllevy/	The AHA Guy at AHAthat	2, 94, 128
Patricia Iyer https://www.linkedin.com/in/patiyer/	President of The Pat Iyer Group	23, 106, 107
Dr. Rachel MK Headley https://www.linkedin.com/in/dr-rachel-mk-headley/	Senior Partner/CEO of Rose Group International, Speaker, Author, Mensa Scientist	9, 64, 79
Sheila A. Anderson https://www.linkedin.com/in/sheilamooreanderson/	Personal Brand Strategist, Author, Speaker	14, 75, 88
Shep Hyken https://www.linkedin.com/in/shephyken/	Chief Amazement Officer of Shepard Presentations	32, 40, 61, 92
Tina Greenbaum https://www.linkedin.com/in/tinagreenbaum/	Transformational Business Coach to Optimal Performance Specialist	4, 36, 55, 115
Todd Williams https://www.linkedin.com/in/todd-m-williams-68b1903/?locale=sr_BA	Sr. Managing Director/Partner at Dillon Kane Group	44, 45, 59, 87
Tony Alessandra https://www.linkedin.com/in/tonyalessandra/	Founder & CVO of Assessments24x7.com	42, 51, 67
Tricia Benn https://www.linkedin.com/in/triciabenn/	General Manager of the C-Suite Network and the Hero Club	19, 111
Wally Hauck https://www.linkedin.com/in/wally-hauck-phd-csp-21749a7/	President of Optimum Leadership	39, 50, 69, 117

About the Authors

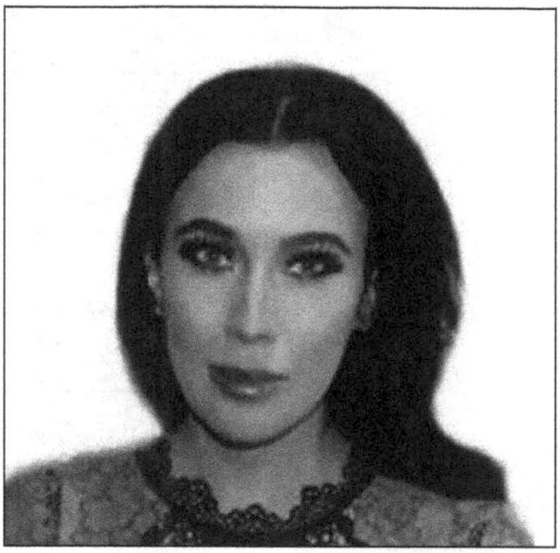

Lindsey Hayzlett http://aha.pub/LindseyHayzlett is the General Manager for C-Suite Network's Thought Leadership. She oversees business development for The Hero Club, C-Suite Network Advisors, C-Suite TV, and C-Suite Radio. Lindsey is a true asset to the C-Suite Network and its members. She is passionately driven to help them become as successful as possible in their respective areas of expertise.

Lindsey also plays an essential role within the sister companies, The Hero Club and Tall Grass Public Relations. She has spent ten years aiding business development and publicity for prominent speakers, celebrities, TV show and podcast hosts, 250-plus well-known executive consultants, and various brands, including Bloomberg Television, Miss Universe Organization, and NBC.

Mitchell Levy http://aha.pub/MitchellLevy, TEDx speaker (http://MitchellLevy.com), is The AHA Guy and CEO at AHAthat and publisher of THiNKaha (http://thinkaha.com) who empowers Thought Leaders to share their genius. He is an international best-selling author with sixty-two business books and a sought-after speaker on thought leadership and creating AHAmessages.

Mitchell's passion is helping entrepreneurs, business owners, and C-Suite Executives get known as thought leaders and become best-selling authors with the AHA platform. His focus is getting his authors recognized as the go-to experts in their field and using the AHA platform to get on stages, get past gatekeepers, and increase revenue.

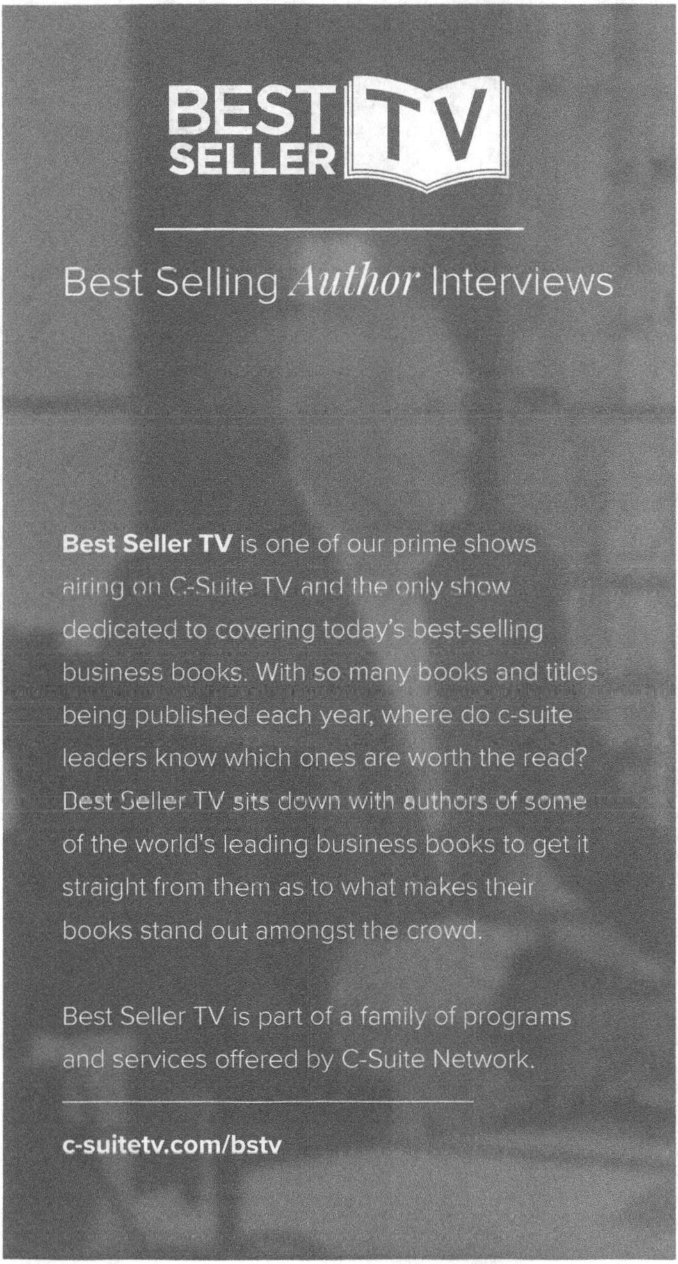
BEST SELLER TV
Best Selling Author Interviews
Best Seller TV is one of our prime shows airing on C-Suite TV and the only show dedicated to covering today's best-selling business books. With so many books and titles being published each year, where do c-suite leaders know which ones are worth the read? Best Seller TV sits down with authors of some of the world's leading business books to get it straight from them as to what makes their books stand out amongst the crowd.
Best Seller TV is part of a family of programs and services offered by C-Suite Network.
c-suitetv.com/bstv

.CEO
Own the Most *Exclusive*
Domain in Business
ClaimYour.CEO

AHAthat™

AHAthat makes it easy to share, author, and promote content. There are over 46,000 AHA messages™ by thought leaders from around the world that you can share in seconds for free on Twitter, Facebook, LinkedIn and Google+.

For those who want to author their own book, we have a 3-step, time-tested proven process, that allows you to write your AHAbook™ of 140 digestible, bite-sized morsels and 5 - 8 blog posts. Once your content is on AHAthat, you have a customized link that you can use to have your fans/advocates share your content and help you grow your network.

- Start sharing: **https://AHAthat.com**
- Start authoring: **https://AHAthat.com/Author**

Please go directly to this book in AHAthat and share each AHAmessage socially at **http://aha.pub/CSuiteExecutivesGuide.**

Printed in the USA
CPSIA information can be obtained
at www.ICGtesting.com
LVHW010015040224
770875LV00010B/935

9 781616 993016